WE ARE ALL STARTERS

A MANIFESTO TO RENEW OURSELVES AND OUR NATION

BY VICTOR W. HWANG

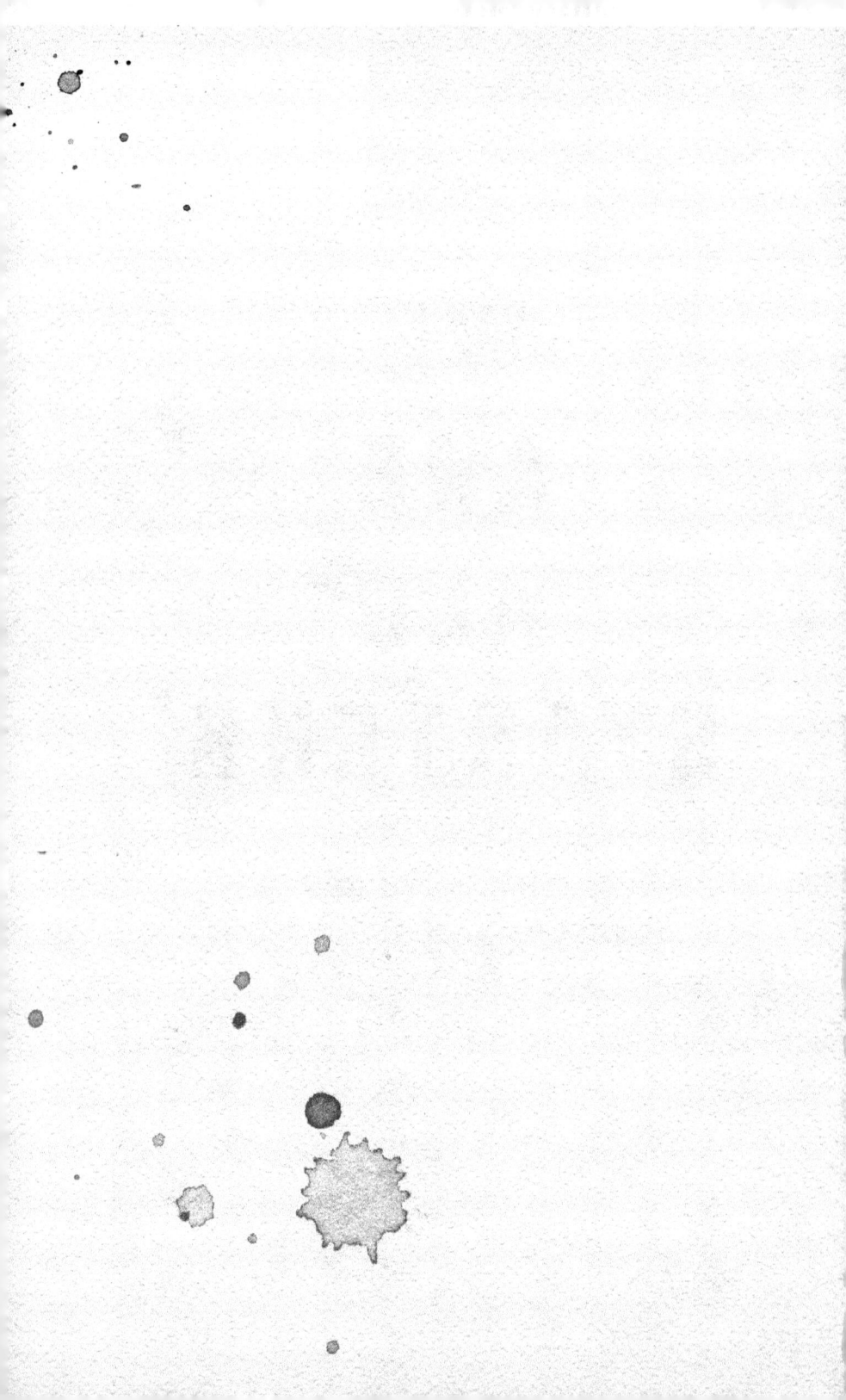

CONTENTS

WHY

We face a crisis of the moment, with a scale of human suffering unthinkable not long ago. Loved ones have perished. Injustices pierce our souls. And with breathtaking speed, millions of our jobs have been displaced, our businesses shuttered, our supply chains of vital goods and services disrupted. Jolted into shock, we now realize just how fragile we were all along.

Getting back to normal is not enough. Our fragility today is the accumulation of decades of choices. We built a system where we dismissed - as the inevitable cost of progress - vast inequities, falling mobility, epidemic rates of depression and hopelessness, and shortened life expectancy. Things are even worse for many of us based on where we live, our skin color or chromosomes, or who we were born to.

We can and must rebuild better. The origin of jobs and prosperity - like the source of a great river - is the creation of new businesses. All great rivers start as small streams. "Little" guys and gals start "little" ideas that can eventually grow, creating value for all of us.

We rebuild by putting those little people - our starters - first. By lifting our starters, we lift our communities. By lifting our communities, we lift our nation.

We are all starters. All of us are born with an innate "right to start," to make an idea into reality. It's time to unleash that right in all of us. That means breaking down barriers, and giving people resources to adapt, start, and grow. That will help millions of us find alternative incomes, restart closed businesses, and open new businesses to provide needed things.

We are proud to launch a nonprofit campaign – called Right to Start – to rebuild the American economy by putting starters first. We seek to do that by changing minds, policies, and communities.

Entrepreneurial opportunity ignites economic justice. Our work is urgent. To begin renewal, we will fight for these "shovel-ready" policies at federal, state, and local levels:

› To create a level playing field and less red tape, we should immediately eliminate startup costs, liberate workers from former employers, cut tax hassles, and dedicate government contracts to young businesses.

› To equalize access to the right kinds of capital everywhere, we should quickly expand capital for young businesses, spur local financial innovation, and make fundraising easier.

› To expand know-how to start businesses, we should promptly expand access to entrepreneurial learning through local providers and libraries.

> To democratize the ability to take risks, we should rapidly make healthcare more portable and defer student loan payments.

Join us at www.righttostart.org.

It's time to start.

Love,

June 2020

PREAMBLE

"I hear America singing, the varied carols I hear...
Each singing what belongs to him or her and to none else...
Singing with open mouths their strong melodious songs."
Walt Whitman

I know the raw muscle of America's dreams. I have heard the countless stories of our struggles and hopes – from scrappy sidewalk vendors to renegade retailers, urban farmers to suburban makers, starry-eyed tech startups to steely-eyed parolees, inventors making gadgets to children making bracelets. I have stood in our musty garages, converted living rooms, frenzied warehouses, and makeshift workspaces across this land, in our tiniest towns and our giant metroplexes, across 50 states plus territories, to hear those stories.

Those little corporate headquarters almost never make headlines, but they are where millions of us start businesses, launch new projects, or simply earn livelihoods. I have felt my heart swell, inspired by our triumphs. I have also fractured inside, watching tears flow from grown adults looking into the abyss. Our nation is made of all those songs. I have been privileged to spend more than two decades immersed in the lives of thousands of entrepreneurs. I write to share with you what I have seen, what I have learned, what I hope for our country.

America is the quintessential startup nation. It was born out of a crazy aspiration in its time – that it might be possible to build a society where each of us is the equal of any other, where each is master of their own future, where each can make of themselves what they dream. It's easy to forget – amid crises of the day – we live in the grandest experiment in the history of the world. While our startup nation has always faced challenges, and has admittedly not always lived up to its own ideals, we have never stopped striving towards a more perfect union. Almost 250 years later, we can look back, take pride in our progress, acknowledge humbly the gaps, and know where we must go.

THE RIGHT TO START

For decades, America appeared to many to gleam. We have achieved technological marvels of which our nation's founders could not possibly have dreamed. Massive efficiencies of scale move money, goods, and talent seemingly at will, with a few clicks. Low unemployment and soaring stock markets suggested a society that should be content. But the numbers deceived us. We were not prepared for the future that was imminent.

A moment of crisis is now upon us, with so many lives cut down and injustices laid bare. Yet that crisis has also exposed a deeper underlying crisis - an economic one - as millions of us lose jobs without foreseeable incomes, as millions of our businesses close shop indefinitely, as formerly dependable goods and services vanish when we need them most. Perhaps the greatest shock is how fragile we were all along. Our system had long been hanging by a string, ready to snap.

We overlooked signals of impending economic crisis for decades, because we were looking at the wrong things. We believed those who said that aggregate numbers - like corporate profits, stock markets, GDP, employment-in-any-job, and maintaining cheap goods - were what mattered. But those indicators are inadequate. They can trend up while millions of us suffer silently, while our system turns fragile, and the rest of us fall complacent.

We were distracted from seeing symptoms of the economic crisis-to-come. Vast inequalities between haves and have-nots. Falling rates of mobility. Dead-end jobs. Epidemic rates of depression and hopelessness. Enduring racial inequities. Fragmenting communities. Lowered life expectancy. Low trust in our institutions and each other. And an increasing sense of purposelessness. The experience can be even worse, depending on our zip codes, our skin color, our chromosomes, or who our parents are.

While looking at the macroeconomy in the abstract, we neglected the individualized economies experienced by those we care dearest about, in our families, neighborhoods, and communities. With the suffering now so great, neglect is no longer an option.

But it's in those individualized economies - instead of the macro economy - where real lives are lived, where we also find hope. The source of that hope is the *Right to Start*. We are all born with the fundamental "right to start" our own ideas and make them real, create our value in the world, and determine our economic destinies. It's a right that's always existed in us and everyone we know, but has never been purposefully articulated.

We are all starters. We are all askers of the question, "Dare I ding the universe?" That's the original promise of America. The right is innate to all of us - whether as an entrepreneur working 15-hour days to build a dream business, a family member kickstarting a project, a grandparent selling their craftwork online, an inventor making a gadget in their garage, a single parent doing a side gig to make ends meet, a friend silently striving to break generational poverty, or a child selling lemonade on the neighborhood corner.

That's what Walt Whitman meant when he heard America singing. Every one of us who starts their own thing is part of a larger choir.

For years, a movement to support the Right to Start has been building quietly, gaining momentum and success, and is finally coming into maturity. The evidence is unambiguous. For each of us, the Right to Start brings dignity, autonomy, and opportunity. At scale, the Right drives prosperity through community renewal, job growth, greater productivity, and economic justice.

Now – as we recover from crisis – it's time for this movement to reveal itself into the open, to show a path for our nation to renew itself, to reopen businesses that have shuttered, to right historical wrongs, and to build a new national civic infrastructure that ignites the Right to Start for everyone, everywhere.

HOW WE GOT HERE

We face an economic crisis of our own making. For the past half century, we struck a grand agreement, believing that lifting up the biggest of us was the same as lifting up all of us. Many of our leaders - politicians, economists, businesspeople - embraced that belief. And the rest of us were complicit, or at least complacent. Giant companies would provide more than enough for everyone, we assumed. Our economy today is the product of that counterfeit consensus.

Today, we are gripped in a system working as it was designed: to supercharge the big players, while ignoring the rest of us trying to make something of ourselves. The result: a fragile, unstable system, set to shatter.

We witnessed America's zeal for giant companies in the contest for Amazon's second headquarters. 238 cities offered billions of dollars in incentives to import jobs from outside their communities. But all along, there was a better, surer, cheaper way. The answer was, and always is, us. The evidence shows that entrepreneurs starting and growing new businesses - not big businesses grabbing subsidies and headlines - are the source of almost all job growth[1] and increased productivity[2] for our nation.

Little newcomers, taken as a whole, contribute more to economic prosperity than big incumbents. One thousand Davids can be more powerful than any Goliath.[3] And every Goliath was once a David too.

If you allow a system for the biggest companies to thrive, while ignoring the newcomers, the voices of the biggest will dominate and eventually control the system, including its policies. That outcome can happen from mere neglect, not necessarily malice. Big companies succeed by becoming more efficient, cutting salaries and other costs as needed to increase profits – that's their job. However, their job does not have to equate our national policy.

The system is tilted in favor of incumbents, against newcomers. It's tilted, in effect, against job growth, increased productivity, and economic resilience for all of us.

Why, for instance, should it be that a large corporation can raise $10 billion in a day, while one of our promising entrepreneurs can take months to raise $10,000 if at all? Why is limited liability an elite privilege that most of us aren't able to utilize? Why does the system spend $34 billion in workforce training to teach job skills for large companies, but next to nothing to teach us to create our own jobs?

Why does $20 billion in economic development funding flow to subsidize large companies that least need the money,[4] while a relative pittance goes to our new businesses that create almost all the net new jobs? Why should big players with lesser products be able to wipe out little players with better products, without a fair fight? Why does unemployment insurance merely serve as a safety net for the newly unemployed, instead of a springboard to help them start their own businesses? Why do inventors lose their life savings protecting inventions from large corporations? Why do government contracts routinely go to established businesses instead of fueling startups?

Our choices as a society led us here. The system has hindered the flow of entrepreneurial activity by adding barriers that accumulate over time, like pebbles build into a dam. Such barriers are many, and include: regulatory burdens, lack of capital access, educational inadequacy, healthcare uncertainty, inequitable taxation, crippling student debt, social network breakdowns, systemic biases against certain groups, anti-competitive markets, bureaucratic red tape, poor support for parenthood, antiquated workforce training, punitive immigration rules, broken patent systems, and misplaced economic development. The list goes on.

Because of this bias against "the small," we have seen a massive decline in American economic dynamism for decades.[5] The decline shows up in many ways in our lives. We are facing a *startup slump*, with the lowest recorded rates of new business starts in over four decades, and businesses closing about as fast as they are starting across almost all sectors. Small business financing under $100,000 – engine fuel for the starting entrepreneur – is nearly impossible to obtain for most of us.[6] Government favors big businesses over little ones, according to 66% of entrepreneurs.[7] More people are stuck in dead-ends, as fewer than 2% of us will start businesses in the next six months, despite that 62% of us have a dream business in mind,[8] 67% are disengaged in our current jobs,[9] and 41% would quit our jobs and start our own business in six months if we could.[10]

Our education systems are failing our future, with only 34% of high school seniors feeling engaged at school and 74% of our college graduates saying they feel unprepared for the real world.[11] Meanwhile, up to 54 million Americans will need to change occupations due to technology and automation in the coming decade.[12] And that was before the pandemic. Our situation is even more urgent now.

Circumstances are even worse for certain segments of us. Businesses founded by women and people of color start smaller and grow slower.[13] Black-owned businesses earn on average about 10% of the revenue of white-owned businesses.[14] Rural areas grapple with 47% of their adult population unemployed or not seeking jobs.[15] Deep inequities so pervade American life, many of us hardly even blink.

Ironically, we are more powerful as individuals than ever in some ways. We have technological tools that enable each of us - with mere fingertips - to access vast information, contact almost anyone anywhere, and transform virtually any idea into reality through the steps of concept, design, prototype, manufacture, distribution, marketing, and sales, often without even leaving our homes. But we are burdened with an economic and governance system stuck in the industrial past, one that condones lasting inequities, one that doesn't respect what we are capable of today.

As a society, we are not ready for the economic future that is already upon us. We are behind the curve.

Fortunately, there is a solution in plain sight. And it draws inspiration from America's original promise.

WHAT WE REALIZE

We are born to be starters, makers, doers, dreamers. That spirit has driven our progress as a human species. To improve the world around us, we create, invent, build, launch, construct, design, explore, and venture forth.

Each of us has a fundamental right to start our own thing, realize an idea, create something of value, forge a unique path, be master of our future. It's not just about entrepreneurship in the narrowest business sense. It's the right for all of us to be entrepreneurial and shape the destiny of our own lives.

That simplest of ideas - that all of us have the Right to Start - is basic to the human condition. When that Right is widespread, prosperity ripples across millions of lives in the form of jobs, productivity, dynamism, and opportunity.

All great things start small. Big rivers start as streams. Big trees start as saplings. "Little" guys and gals start "little" businesses that can grow into great ones, creating value for all of us.

But entrepreneurs can't do it alone. Rather, entrepreneurship is a community endeavor. We need to be surrounded by other people who support our journeys, because all new ideas start small and grow through webs of human relationships. Everyone can be a potential customer, partner, employee, referral, contractor, service provider, supplier, investor, or simply a friend who lends a hand.

It's fitting that entrepreneurial networks are often called "eco-systems." They are environments – like natural rainforests – that are dynamic and interconnected, where serendipitous value emerges from diverse interactions between all of us, where our whole is greater than the sum of our parts.

Fortunately, ecosystems can be built. Many of our communities have already begun.

Indeed, every community already starts with the basic ingredients they need. Building ecosystems is accessible to any community – no matter the size or shape, whether bounded by neighborhood, town, city, state, or region, or whether defined by demographic, socioeconomic, or geographic lines. And unlike other methods to grow economies – which often require significant cash or physical infrastructure – building ecosystems takes little cost to get started.

There's an open door to join.[16] One can change the world for the cost of a cup of coffee.

By building ecosystems, we unleash our starters.

By unleashing our starters, we unleash the latent economic might of our communities.[17]

By unleashing our communities, we lift our nation.

WHERE WE START

We aren't starting from scratch. To promote the Right to Start, we can build on our nation's story and a growing support infrastructure that's been mostly hidden from view so far.

When our nation was founded, its economy was dominated by entrepreneurs, even though that word didn't exist yet. The majority were tradespeople, craftspeople, merchants, farmers, or other independent workers. Sadly, many of us were excluded and exploited - our African-American and Native American brethren suffered injustices for which we must still atone.

Yet for most, the Right to Start was suffused in ordinary life. It was simply assumed.

Our nation's founders never experienced industrialization and didn't envision companies employing vast numbers of people, as they do now. And they certainly didn't envision that so many of us would depend on such large companies for basic security. After all, the Boston Tea Party was an entrepreneurs' rebellion, protesting against restraints on ordinary Americans trading and making a living. Historically, the Right to Start was implicit - albeit imperfectly - in the promise of America.

Despite centuries of striving to form a more perfect union, the Right to Start still exists in our national DNA. The spirit just needs rekindling, for a new era, for a new citizenry.

To renew it, we must remember as a nation what it is to climb from the bottom to the top. We must honor the efforts of those pushing against the current. We must support those who propel frontiers forward. We must renew the idea that the origin of prosperity begins with common people, not large incumbents. And this time, we must do so inclusively and with equity, so all of us ascend together.

America's entrepreneurial infrastructure has grown quietly, but is now surprisingly vast. Although that infrastructure is mostly invisible - unlike the shiny structures of big businesses - it already stretches from coast to coast, across all 50 states, D.C., and territories.

I've been to many of those spaces - both live and virtual - where we gather to meet, share knowledge, and help one another. They are as inspiring as they are varied. They can be simple meetups, like coffee shops, local watering holes, or online forums where we exchange information. They are local gatherings like 1 Million Cups, now in over 160 communities weekly, with 150,000 participants last year. They are national events where champions for entrepreneurs convene, like the Kauffman Foundation's ESHIP Summits, involving over 1,200 leaders from every state, and the Startup Champions Network, made of over 100 ecosystem builders. We can count well over 1,000 organizations, 300 community colleges, and 200 universities teaching hands-on skills to entrepreneurs, mentoring those who aspire by passing knowledge forward, spinning out technologies, and providing starters with coworking spaces, incubators, accelerators, maker spaces, and design labs.

To renew ourselves and our nation, we must now translate that entrepreneurial infrastructure into a civic infrastructure that is permanent. We begin with a strong foundation to do so, probably more so than any country in the world. Our special heritage and existing assets mean we don't have to begin at zero.

We have a running start.

We are ready to rise.

WHO WE ARE

Whether or not that future arrives is up to us. No savior is coming to the rescue. No superhero is popping into the next movie scene. America's greatest venture is actually you and me. We are the ones who will renew its promise. We are the leaders we've been waiting for.

There's a simple formula to remember that idea: 3 + 997 = 1,000

Every month out of 1,000 of us, only 3 start new businesses. But those 3 can't succeed on their own. The success of the 3 depends on what the other 997 do – how a community wraps around its starters. Each of us in the 997 can contribute in our own way to enhance the success of the 3. And hopefully grow that number.

How can each of us support the Right to Start in our daily lives? At the simplest level, we can be an early customer for a new business, especially when times are tough. Try out that new store or restaurant in the neighborhood. Support that crowdfund project launched by a friend. Shop at that small online store, instead of the giant one.

You might not like what you get sometimes, and that's OK. Then again, you might actually love it. Something unique, not mass-produced. But in any event, you gave someone who started a fair shot.

We can do other easy things too:

› Make useful introductions.

› Share your expertise.

› Mentor someone.

› Provide feedback.

› Connect starters to potential partners or employees.

› Introduce them to people with useful skills.

› Convene starters so they can help each other.

› Teach entrepreneurial skills to the next generation.

› Give emotional support for the lonely journey.

We can also advocate for policy change. While political leaders want to hear from citizens, most entrepreneurs and other starters are often too busy (or too cash-strapped) to advocate for themselves. So be a voice for the voiceless starters. Talk to political leaders, and let them know the Right to Start deserves their support.

If you aren't one of the 3, then be an amazing member of the 997. That's how we level the playing field for starters, by tapping the full power of all of us in the 1,000.

Each of us contains the superhero we need inside. Each of us can lay a brick in the civic infrastructure.

None of us should be a bystander.

All of us matter.

WHAT WE BELIEVE

To change a nation, we must first change hearts. The Right to Start is more than just an economic or political strategy – it is a philosophy grounded in a set of beliefs about how the world should be.

When fighting for the Right to Start, here are six principles that steer us forward:

1. Everyone has a fundamental Right to Start.
We are born to be starters, makers, doers, dreamers. The Right to Start is granted to each of us at birth, just like other recognized rights to speech, worship, and assembly. It's time to refresh the Right to Start for the modern era, to make it explicit instead of implicit, so it won't ever be taken for granted again. The Right should be enshrined as a fundamental tenet in law, governance, and business that cannot be suppressed or taken away. America can and should be a startup nation, once again and forever.

2. We must protect and nourish starters.
Society should provide equal access to resources for all of us to start and grow. America is richer in its latent talent than in any other resource. But we are only as rich as the littlest among us is allowed to flourish. Each one of us whose Right to Start is suppressed or neglected is a small death for all of us. The purpose of government should be to protect

and nourish everyone's Right to Start, so our brilliance can shine, so we can leverage the full talents of our people in our unparalleled diversity.

3. To level the playing field, tilt it.

We Americans don't seek favors, but we demand an equal shot. Playing fields naturally tilt in favor of the biggest players. To keep the playing field level, we must intentionally tilt it the other way. Every corporate giant was a startup in the past. Each wave of newcomers deserves fresh chances to succeed. Incumbents should pay it forward, not prevent newcomers from playing the game. A fair game is one that's tilted positively to empower every newcomer's Right to Start.

4. Renewal comes bottom-up.

Communities can be transformed by lifting people. The Right to Start provides a path to renew our communities, whether a neighborhood, city, region, state, or other category, as new enterprises start and grow. Although traditional policies often focus on big institutions and big numbers, those tactics no longer yield desired results. Instead, more communities across the country are focusing their strategies on home-grown starters, because it works. Every community can grab that powerful change lever in plain sight. Now it's time to pull it.

5. Grow ecosystems to grow economies.

Prosperity comes by people breaking barriers, fostering trust, and bridging differences to tackle challenges together.

The Right to Start thrives in ecosystems where people collaborate, ideas flow, and value grows. The Right withers in their absence. Imagine an ecosystem as an interconnected, invisible web of human relationships, becoming more powerful as it gets more interwoven. The Right to Start thrives when that web connects us together better. Ecosystems are an invisible infrastructure we can build intentionally.

6. All of us matter.

Every big idea starts small, and needs help to grow. The old economy said, we were cogs, we didn't really matter. The Right to Start says, we are everything we need. The formula $3 + 997 = 1,000$ is built on that idea. Some people start, others help, but we all matter. Everything worth building, we build together. Throughout history, it wasn't the famous or powerful who truly shaped the world. The real difference has always been individuals - like us - pooling our abilities together.

HOW WE ADVANCE

The Right to Start is a simple idea, but with profound connotations. It means we all possess the spark to change things. It means our communities have tinder to ignite. It means America retains DNA from our past that is key to our future.

As we rebuild, it is time to permanently imprint the Right to Start in our system, so it gets indelibly etched, so it will never be taken for granted again. By enshrining the Right to Start in our communities and across federal, state, and local policies, we will renew America for the modern era.

Let us fight to make starting a priority in American life. We are proud to launch a new nonprofit campaign called Right to Start. The campaign seeks to rebuild the American economy by putting starters first. That means creating a national infrastructure that unleashes the innate Right to Start in all of us. The effort is based in a 501(c)(3) for education, advocacy, and other charitable efforts, with an affiliated 501(c)(4) for social welfare and targeted policy work.

We will fight to enshrine the Right to Start permanently in our economic and governmental system by these three strategies:

› **Change minds.** Win the battle of ideas by shifting our nation's conversation to celebrate starters and elevate the Right to Start as critical to American renewal.

› **Change policies.** Advocate for awareness, adoption, and implementation of policies to enshrine the Right to Start at all levels of our system.

› **Change communities.** Engage ordinary Americans in lifting their communities at the grassroots through simple actions that create awareness, influence policies, and recruit advocates for the Right to Start.

We need you in this effort. There's a guide for our steps ahead. It's called "America's New Business Plan" and is backed by a coalition of over 160 organizations.[18] We created this plan during my tenure at the Kauffman Foundation. It's the most comprehensive policy roadmap ever written putting entrepreneurs front and center to grow our shared prosperity. It provides practical, actionable policy ideas grouped in four pillars:

› **Opportunity.** A level playing field and less red tape.

› **Funding.** Equal access to the right kind of capital everywhere.

› **Knowledge.** The know-how to start a business.

› **Support.** The ability for all to take risks.

America's New Business Plan proposes 14 recommendations with 43 specific points, provides valuable data and case studies, and gives action checklists of 25 to-do's for federal, state, and local policymakers to follow.

To aid our nation's immediate recovery from the pandemic, we are proposing "Ready to Start" policies – inspired by America's New Business Plan – to implement right away. They would help millions of displaced workers find new incomes, restart closed businesses, open new businesses to provide needed goods and services, and diversify our supply chains. That policy roadmap can be found at the end of this document.

Thus we begin a campaign for the soul of our nation. The Right to Start is more than just a basket of policies. Taken as a whole, the ideas constitute an ideological revolution.

Talk to your leaders about these ideas. Engage with your family, friends, and neighbors. Win hearts and minds, one conversation at a time.

When we vocalize, we'll wake our fellow Americans.

When we mobilize, we'll shake America.

WHERE WE GO

"O, yes,
I say it plain,
America never was America to me,
And yet I swear this oath—
America will be!"

Langston Hughes

As we recover from tragedy, we can make a better tomorrow. Getting back to normal is not enough. It's now up to millions of us to rise up and define our own future. We have the power to create a starter-centric nation.

We have our world to win. We have our dreams to lose.

Let us now build the nation we envision, the one that fulfills its original promise, the one where poet Langston Hughes dreamed "America will be."

Where each of us who asks for a fair shot, gets that fair shot. Where each of us who craves dignity, can stand tall as master of our own destiny. Where each of us with just an idea and inspiration, is sure to find what we need to succeed.

Where the Right to Start is not just a distant notion reserved for someone else, but a practical reality for any one of us who dreams a dream, determines to venture forth, a gleam in our eye, a bounce in our stride.

Where any of us can stand tall and shout, "I am here. I create the future. I make the world. I am a starter."

We owe it to our families, our friends, our communities, our nation. And our descendants who follow.

It's time to start. It's time to fight.

America, let me hear you sing.

Love, Victor

READY TO START:
A ROADMAP FOR RECOVERY

We must rise to the moment. Millions of small businesses have shuttered, laying off millions of Americans. Nationwide, there is desperate need to help people find alternative income, restart closed businesses, open new businesses to provide missing goods and services, and diversify supply chains. Entrepreneurship has become an urgent priority of economic recovery and justice.

America is still a nation of starters, makers, doers, dreamers. To renew ourselves and our economy, we must unleash the potential of our people. Everyone with a business idea has a "right to start" and should be able to access what they need, whether as startups, freelancers, independent contractors, sole proprietors, or cooperatives. That's how we create new jobs, productivity, and opportunity. That's how we recover as a nation. We propose these "shovel-ready" policies at federal, state, and local levels:

OPPORTUNITY
A level playing field and less red tape

1. **Zero barriers to start.** Eliminate all registration costs, minimum income taxes, and licensing fees to cut red tape for new businesses at start and in their early years.

2. **Free to compete.** Prohibit noncompete agreements that prevent Americans from starting new businesses because they're locked out by former employers.

3. **Cut tax hassles.** Allow businesses to defer federal and state income tax deadlines, or to skip filing income taxes for a year if net income is below $5,000.

4. **Access to contracts.** Dedicate 5% of government procurement dollars to businesses under 5 years old.

FUNDING
Equal access to the right kind of capital everywhere.

5. **More early-stage capital.** Help displaced workers use unemployment benefits to start their own businesses. Pass an updated version of the State Small Business Credit Initiative, which previously invested $1.5B to spur $8.4B in small business lending.

6. **Spur local financial innovation.** Create Entrepreneurial Capital Catalyst Grants to invest in starting and restarting businesses underserved by the capital marketplace.

7. **Easier fundraising.** Pass the Small Business Borrowers' Bill of Rights. Pass the SEC's proposed rule changes to harmonize and simplify startup fundraising.

KNOWLEDGE
The know-how to start a business.

8. **Drive local learning.** Redirect 5% ($2.7B) of workforce training and economic development funding into helping Americans start businesses through local entrepreneurial support organizations.

9. **Easy access.** Strengthen local libraries as hubs of knowledge and digital tools for entrepreneurs.

SUPPORT
The ability for all to take risks.

10. **Healthcare mobility.** Provide tax support for health insurance portability to Americans starting their own businesses. Aggregate entrepreneurs into state-wide group insurance plans.

11. **Debt relief.** Defer student loan payments for Americans who take the risk to start businesses.

For more policy ideas to help entrepreneurs drive prosperity, see America's New Business Plan at **www.startusupnow.org**. Right to Start is a campaign to build the American economy by putting starters first. We seek to achieve that by changing minds, policies, and communities. The organization Right to Start is a 501(c)3 nonprofit, which is affiliated with a 501(c)4 nonprofit called Right to Start Fund.

For more info, visit **www.righttostart.org** or contact **info@ righttostart.org**

ENDNOTES

1 Haltiwanger, John, Ron Jarmin, and Javier Miranda, "Who Creates Jobs? Small vs. Large vs. Young" (U.S. Census Bureau Center for Economic Studies, August 2010). https://www.nber.org/papers/w16300.pdf

2 Foster, Lucia, Cheryl Grim, John Haltiwanger, Zoltan Wolf, "Firm innovation and productivity: Searching for Black Holes" (CEPR Policy Portal, June 2018). https://voxeu.org/article/firm-innovation-and-productivity

3 See, e.g., KC SourceLink, "We Create: Making KC America's Most Entrepreneurial City" (website on April 13, 2020): Kansas City entrepreneurs created over 75,000 jobs over 5 years, compared with Amazon's promised 50,000 jobs over 5 years. https://www.kcsourcelink.com/wecreate/jobs

4 Slattery, Cailin and Owen Zidar, "Evaluating State and Local Business Tax Incentives" (NBER Working Paper No. 26603, January 2020) https://www.nber.org/papers/w26603; as referenced in Rabouin, Dion, "Company tax incentives don't spur economic growth" (Axios, January 7, 2020). https://www.axios.com/company-tax-incentives-dont-spur-economic-growth-2de3d-fbc-ca98-4a48-aa93-2cacb3695a5d.html

5 Economic Innovation Group, "Dynamism in Retreat: Consequences for Regions, Markets, and Workers" (February 2017). https://eig.org/wp-content/uploads/2017/07/Dynamism-in-Retreat-A.pdf

6 Survey by Revolve Capital in Raleigh-Durham, North Carolina (2018).

7 Kauffman Foundation and Global Strategy Group, "Kauffman Foundation Entrepreneurship Survey" (2018).

8 "America's Small Business Development Centers and the Center for Generational Kinetics, "America's Voice on Small Business," (May 2017). https://americassbdc.org/wp-content/uploads/2017/05/White-Paper-GenStudy-6-1-2017.pdf

9 Royal, Ken, "Heard of the U.S. Quit Rate? Win the War for Talent Now" (July 12, 2019). https://www.gallup.com/workplace/260564/heard-quit-rate-win-war-talent.aspx

10 America's Small Business Development Centers and the Center for Generational Kinetics, "America's Voice on Small Business" (May 2017).

11 Musto, Pete, "US College Students Feel Unprepared for 'Real World'" (VOA, October 6, 2016), citing Association of American Colleges and Universities (AACU) survey. https://www.voanews.com/usa/us-college-students-feel-unprepared-real-world

12 Manyika, James, et al., "Jobs lost, jobs gained: What the future of work will mean for jobs, skills, and wages" (McKinsey Global Institute, November 2017). https://www.mckinsey.com/featured-insights/future-of-work/jobs-lost-jobs-gained-what-the-future-of-work-will-mean-for-jobs-skills-and-wages

13 Kauffman Foundation, "Zero Barriers: Three Mega Trends Shaping the Future of Entrepreneurship" (2017), citing calculations from U.S. Census Bureau Annual Survey of Entrepreneurs. https://www.kauffman.org/wp-content/uploads/2019/12/state_of_entrepreneurship_address_report_2017.pdf

14 Myers, Spectra and Pamela Chan, "Stuck from the Start: The Financial Challenges of Low-and Moderate-Income African-American Entrepreneurs in the South" (Prosperity Now, 2017), citing SBA 2012 Survey of Business Owners. https://prosperitynow.org/sites/default/files/PDFs/07-2017_stuck_from_the_start.pdf

15 U.S. Chamber Technology Engagement Center, "Unlocking the Digital Potential of Rural America" (2019), study commissioned by Amazon. https://americaninnovators.com/wp-content/uploads/2019/03/Unlocking-the-Digital-Potential-of-Rural-America.pdf

16 Feld, Brad, Startup Communities, Wiley, Hoboken, NJ (2013) (ecosystem building is bottom-up); OECD, Entrepreneurial ecosystems and growth-oriented entrepreneurship (2013) (institutions support networks). http://www.oecd.org/cfe/leed/entrepreneurialecosystemsandgrowthorientedentrepreneurshipworkshop-netherlands.htm; Álvarez, C., Urbano, D., & Amorós, J. E. GEM research: achievements and challenges. Small Business Economics (2014), 42(3), 445-465 (building social capital); Flora, C. B., & Flora, J. L.. "Entrepreneurial social infrastructure: A necessary ingredient." The Annals of the American Academy of Political and Social Science (1993), 529(1), 48-58; Krueger, Norris, "The cognitive infrastructure of opportunity emergence", Entrepreneurship Theory and Practice (2000), Vol. 24 No. 3, pp. 5-23 (building intangible infrastructure); Krueger, Norris, "OECD thematic paper on entrepreneurial education in practice: Part 1, the entrepreneurial mindset." (Published online, 2015). http://www.oecd.org/cfe/leed/Entrepreneurial-Education-Practice-pt1.pdf

17 DeVol, Ross, et al., "Young Firms Regional Economic Growth: Knowledge-Intensive Firms Critical" (Heartland Forward, May 2020). https://heartlandforward.org/media/pages/young-firms-and-regional-economic-growth/2863128872-1588779952/young-firms_full-report-launch.pdf

18 See https://www.startusupnow.org

THE AUTHOR'S STORY

Victor W. Hwang is an economic growth expert. His ideas have shaped the economic lives of millions of people worldwide. His work has helped over 300 communities, cities, states, companies, and entire countries create greater prosperity.

Victor's path was inspired by his parents, as educators who had to start a business to afford sending him to Harvard. But after the first day of Economics at Harvard, Victor left the class and never returned. He realized that Economics – the way it was taught at elite institutions – was flawed. It didn't account for his parents, and all the ordinary people like them trying to make their way. Victor's life's journey followed from that day. He rejected orthodox economic thinking and searched for answers to the questions, "How can we create prosperity by taking into account everyday people? How do we make a world that doesn't stand in their way?"

Victor became an entrepreneur and started several companies, organizations, and initiatives fighting to remove barriers holding people back. He is founder and CEO of Right to Start, a campaign fighting for the rights of entrepreneurs as a national priority. Previously, he was Vice President of Entrepreneurship at the Kauffman Foundation, the world's leading philanthropy supporting entrepreneurs with an endowment of $2 billion. At Kauffman, he led initiatives that impacted over 200,000 entrepreneurs in 200 cities, including efforts in catalyzing capital formation, transforming economic development practices, launching a national policy roadmap, and funding programs that break barriers for underserved entrepreneurs.

He started a Silicon Valley venture studio that started, invested in, and grew new companies while also advising cities, regions, and countries on growing their innovative economies. Several of their companies were acquired, including a digital technology company where Victor served as Chief Strategy Officer. Another company with technology for safe drinking water won the TechCrunch Disrupt startup competition.

Victor has created two leading conferences on unleashing innovation and entrepreneurship in communities. The Global Innovation Summit became Silicon Valley's leading conference on building innovative economies, with over 1,000 delegates from 50 nations. The ESHIP Summit, during Victor's term at the Kauffman Foundation, became the nation's leading conference on building entrepreneurial communities, with over 1,200 attendees from all 50 states and over 100 mayors and key staff.

National Public Radio named Victor's graduation address to Austin Community College one of "the best commencement speeches ever." He pioneered the metaphor "rainforest" in a business context. He applied it to show how communities can replicate the historical innovation dynamics of Silicon Valley. His co-authored book, *The Rainforest*, was awarded Book of the Year, Gold Medal, by ForeWord Reviews for "a big idea that defines a way of thinking."

Victor can be reached at: **www.victorh.co**